TRA GUYANESE COOKBOOK

AVA BAKER

CONTENTS

MAIN DISHES - MEAT AND SEAFOOD   66

DESSERTS AND SWEETS   88

APPETIZERS AND SNACKS

Pepperpot Pastries

Servings: Makes 12 pastries

Time: 1 hour

Ingredients:

- 2 cups leftover Pepperpot (shredded beef in cassareep sauce)
- 2 sheets puff pastry, thawed
- 1 egg, beaten (for egg wash)

Directions:

1. Preheat the oven to 375°F (190°C).
2. Roll out the puff pastry sheets on a lightly floured surface.

3. Cut the pastry sheets into squares or rectangles, depending on your preference.

4. Place a spoonful of shredded Pepperpot in the center of each pastry square.

5. Fold the pastry over the filling, creating a triangle or rectangle shape. Press the edges to seal.

6. Place the filled pastries on a baking sheet lined with parchment paper.

7. Brush the tops of the pastries with beaten egg for a golden finish.

8. Bake in the preheated oven for 20-25 minutes or until the pastries are puffed and golden brown.

9. Allow the Pepperpot Pastries to cool slightly before serving.

Cassava Fries with Tamarind Dip

Servings: Serves 4

Time: 45 minutes

Ingredients:

- 2 large cassava roots, peeled and cut into fries
- 2 tablespoons olive oil
- 1 teaspoon garlic powder
- 1 teaspoon paprika
- Salt and pepper, to taste

Tamarind Dip:

- 1/2 cup tamarind pulp, soaked in 1/2 cup warm water
- 2 tablespoons honey
- 1 teaspoon soy sauce
- 1/2 teaspoon red pepper flakes (optional)

Directions:

1. Preheat the oven to 425°F (220°C) and line a baking sheet with parchment paper.
2. In a large bowl, toss the cassava fries with olive oil, garlic powder, paprika, salt, and pepper until evenly coated.
3. Arrange the seasoned cassava fries in a single layer on the prepared baking sheet.

4. Bake in the preheated oven for 30-35 minutes or until the fries are golden brown and crispy, flipping them halfway through.

5. While the fries are baking, prepare the tamarind dip. Mix the soaked tamarind pulp, honey, soy sauce, and red pepper flakes (if using) in a bowl until well combined.

6. Once the cassava fries are done, remove them from the oven and let them cool slightly.

7. Serve the cassava fries with the tamarind dip on the side.

Aloo Pie (Potato Turnovers)

Servings: Makes 12 pies

Time: 1 hour

Ingredients:

For the Filling:

- 3 large potatoes, boiled and mashed
- 1 tablespoon oil
- 1 small onion, finely chopped
- 2 cloves garlic, minced
- 1 teaspoon curry powder
- 1/2 teaspoon ground cumin
- 1/2 teaspoon turmeric powder
- Salt and pepper, to taste
- 2 tablespoons chopped cilantro

For the Dough:

- 2 cups all-purpose flour
- 1/2 cup butter, cold and cubed
- 1/2 cup water
- 1/2 teaspoon salt

Directions:

Filling:

1. In a pan, heat oil over medium heat. Add chopped onions and garlic, sauté until softened.
2. Add curry powder, ground cumin, turmeric, salt, and pepper. Cook for an additional 2 minutes.
3. Add the mashed potatoes to the spice mixture and mix well, ensuring the potatoes are coated evenly.
4. Stir in chopped cilantro, then remove the filling from heat and let it cool.

Dough:

1. In a large bowl, combine flour and salt. Add cold, cubed butter, and mix until the mixture resembles coarse crumbs.
2. Gradually add water and knead the dough until it comes together. Wrap the dough in plastic wrap and refrigerate for 30 minutes.

Assembling:

1. Preheat the oven to 375°F (190°C) and line a baking sheet with parchment paper.
2. Roll out the chilled dough on a floured surface and cut into circles using a round cutter.
3. Place a spoonful of the potato filling in the center of each dough circle.

4. Fold the dough over the filling, creating a half-moon shape, and seal the edges using a fork.

5. Place the turnovers on the prepared baking sheet and bake for 20-25 minutes or until golden brown.

Chicken Patties

Servings: Makes 10 patties

Time: 1 hour

Ingredients:

For the Filling:

- 1 lb ground chicken
- 1 tablespoon oil
- 1 small onion, finely chopped
- 2 cloves garlic, minced
- 1 teaspoon curry powder
- 1/2 teaspoon dried thyme
- 1/2 teaspoon paprika
- Salt and pepper, to taste
- 2 tablespoons chopped fresh parsley
- 1/4 cup breadcrumbs

For the Dough:

- 2 cups all-purpose flour
- 1/2 cup unsalted butter, cold and cubed
- 1/2 cup water
- 1/2 teaspoon salt

Directions:

Filling:

1. In a pan, heat oil over medium heat. Add chopped onions and garlic, sauté until softened.
2. Add ground chicken and cook until browned, breaking it apart with a spoon as it cooks.
3. Stir in curry powder, dried thyme, paprika, salt, and pepper. Cook for an additional 5 minutes.
4. Add chopped parsley and breadcrumbs, mix well. Remove the filling from heat and let it cool.

Dough:

1. In a large bowl, combine flour and salt. Add cold, cubed butter, and mix until the mixture resembles coarse crumbs.
2. Gradually add water and knead the dough until it comes together. Wrap the dough in plastic wrap and refrigerate for 30 minutes.

Assembling:

1. Preheat the oven to 375°F (190°C) and line a baking sheet with parchment paper.
2. Roll out the chilled dough on a floured surface and cut into circles using a round cutter.

3. Place a spoonful of the chicken filling in the center of each dough circle.

4. Fold the dough over the filling, creating a half-moon shape, and seal the edges using a fork.

5. Place the patties on the prepared baking sheet and bake for 20-25 minutes or until golden brown.

Plantain Chips with Mango Salsa

Servings: Serves 4

Time: 30 minutes

Ingredients:

For the Plantain Chips:

- 2 ripe plantains, peeled and thinly sliced
- Vegetable oil, for frying
- Salt, to taste

For the Mango Salsa:

- 1 ripe mango, peeled and diced
- 1/2 red onion, finely chopped
- 1 jalapeño, seeded and finely chopped
- 1/4 cup fresh cilantro, chopped
- Juice of 1 lime
- Salt and pepper, to taste

Directions:

Plantain Chips:

1. In a deep pan, heat vegetable oil over medium heat.
2. Fry the plantain slices in batches until golden brown and crispy. Remove with a slotted spoon and drain on paper towels.

3. Sprinkle the hot plantain chips with salt to taste.

Mango Salsa:

1. In a bowl, combine diced mango, chopped red onion, jalapeño, and cilantro.
2. Squeeze lime juice over the mixture and toss gently to combine.
3. Season with salt and pepper to taste.

Dhal Puri Roti

Servings: Makes 10 rotis

Time: 2 hours

Ingredients:

For the Roti Dough:

- 3 cups all-purpose flour
- 1 teaspoon baking powder
- 1/2 teaspoon salt
- Water, as needed

For the Dhal Filling:

- 1 cup split yellow peas (chana dhal), soaked for 2 hours
- 2 cloves garlic, minced
- 1 teaspoon ground turmeric
- 1 teaspoon ground cumin
- Salt, to taste

Directions:

Roti Dough:

1. In a large bowl, combine flour, baking powder, and salt.
2. Gradually add water and knead the dough until it becomes soft and pliable.

3. Divide the dough into 10 equal portions and shape them into balls.

4. Cover the dough balls and let them rest for at least 30 minutes.

Dhal Filling:

1. Rinse the soaked split yellow peas and place them in a pot with enough water to cover. Cook until tender.

2. Drain any excess water from the cooked peas and mash them.

3. Add minced garlic, ground turmeric, ground cumin, and salt to the mashed peas. Mix well to form a smooth filling.

Assembling:

1. Take a dough ball, flatten it, and place a spoonful of the dhal filling in the center.

2. Fold the edges of the dough over the filling, sealing it to form a ball again.

3. Roll out each filled dough ball into a thin, round roti.

Cooking:

1. Heat a griddle or flat pan over medium-high heat.

2. Cook each dhal puri roti on the hot surface, flipping it when bubbles start to form.

3. Brush both sides of the roti with a bit of oil or ghee while cooking until it turns golden brown.

Baiganee (Eggplant Fritters)

Servings: Makes 12 fritters

Time: 45 minutes

Ingredients:

- **1 large eggplant, peeled and sliced into 1/4-inch rounds**
- **1 cup chickpea flour (besan)**
- **1 teaspoon ground cumin**
- **1 teaspoon ground coriander**
- **1/2 teaspoon turmeric powder**
- **1/2 teaspoon chili powder**
- **1/2 teaspoon baking powder**
- **Salt, to taste**
- **Water, as needed**
- **Vegetable oil, for frying**

Directions:

1. **In a bowl, combine chickpea flour, ground cumin, ground coriander, turmeric powder, chili powder, baking powder, and salt.**
2. **Gradually add water to the dry ingredients, whisking continuously until you achieve a smooth, thick batter.**
3. **Heat vegetable oil in a deep pan over medium-high heat for frying.**

4. Dip each eggplant slice into the batter, ensuring it is evenly coated.

5. Carefully place the batter-coated eggplant slices into the hot oil, frying until golden brown on both sides.

6. Use a slotted spoon to remove the baiganee from the oil and place them on paper towels to absorb any excess oil.

Shark and Bake

Servings: Serves 4

Time: 1.5 hours

Ingredients:

For the Fried Shark:

- 1 lb shark fillets
- 1 cup all-purpose flour
- 1 teaspoon paprika
- 1/2 teaspoon garlic powder
- Salt and pepper, to taste
- Vegetable oil, for frying

For the Bake (Bread):

- 3 cups all-purpose flour
- 1 tablespoon sugar
- 1 tablespoon baking powder
- 1/2 teaspoon salt
- Water, as needed
- Vegetable oil, for frying

Toppings and Condiments:

- Shredded lettuce
- Sliced tomatoes

- Sliced cucumbers
- Sliced onions
- Hot pepper sauce
- Tamarind sauce or mango chutney

Directions:

Fried Shark:

1. In a bowl, mix flour, paprika, garlic powder, salt, and pepper.
2. Dredge shark fillets in the seasoned flour mixture, ensuring they are evenly coated.
3. Heat vegetable oil in a pan over medium-high heat.
4. Fry the shark fillets until golden brown and cooked through. Remove and drain on paper towels.

Bake (Bread):

1. In a large bowl, combine flour, sugar, baking powder, and salt.
2. Gradually add water, kneading the dough until it is soft and elastic.
3. Divide the dough into balls and roll each into a flat disc.
4. Heat vegetable oil in a pan over medium heat.
5. Fry the bread until puffed and golden brown, flipping to cook both sides.

Assembling:

1. Cut the fried bake in half horizontally, creating a pocket.

2. Stuff the bake with fried shark fillets and your choice of toppings – shredded lettuce, sliced tomatoes, cucumbers, and onions.

3. Drizzle with hot pepper sauce and tamarind sauce or mango chutney.

Cassava Balls with Shrimp

Servings: Makes 20 balls

Time: 1.5 hours

Ingredients:

For the Cassava Balls:

- 2 cups cassava, peeled, grated, and squeezed to remove excess liquid
- 1 cup cooked and finely chopped shrimp
- 1/2 cup finely chopped onions
- 2 cloves garlic, minced
- 2 tablespoons chopped fresh cilantro
- 1 teaspoon ground cumin
- Salt and pepper, to taste
- Vegetable oil, for frying

For the Dipping Sauce:

- 1/2 cup plain yogurt
- 1 tablespoon chopped fresh mint
- 1 tablespoon lime juice
- Salt, to taste

Directions:

Cassava Balls:

1. In a large bowl, combine grated cassava, chopped shrimp, onions, garlic, cilantro, ground cumin, salt, and pepper.
2. Mix the ingredients thoroughly to form a cohesive mixture.
3. Take a small portion of the mixture and shape it into a ball. Repeat until all the mixture is used.
4. Heat vegetable oil in a pan over medium-high heat for frying.
5. Fry the cassava balls until they are golden brown and crispy on the outside. Drain on paper towels.

Dipping Sauce:

1. In a small bowl, mix together yogurt, chopped mint, lime juice, and salt to taste.
2. Stir until well combined.

Mutton Pholourie

Servings: Makes 30 pholourie

Time: 1.5 hours

Ingredients:

For the Pholourie:

- 1 cup split yellow peas (chana dhal), soaked for 2 hours
- 1 cup all-purpose flour
- 1 teaspoon baking powder
- 1/2 teaspoon ground cumin
- 1/2 teaspoon ground turmeric
- 1/2 teaspoon ground coriander
- 2 cloves garlic, minced
- 1 hot pepper, finely chopped (adjust to taste)
- 1/2 cup finely chopped fresh cilantro
- Salt, to taste
- Water, as needed
- Vegetable oil, for frying

For the Mutton Filling:

- 1 lb mutton, cooked and shredded
- 1 onion, finely chopped
- 2 cloves garlic, minced
- 1 teaspoon ground cumin

- 1 teaspoon curry powder
- 1/2 teaspoon turmeric powder
- Salt and pepper, to taste
- Vegetable oil, for sautéing

Directions:

Pholourie:

1. Rinse the soaked split yellow peas and place them in a blender with a little water. Blend until you get a smooth batter.
2. In a bowl, combine the pea batter, all-purpose flour, baking powder, ground cumin, turmeric, coriander, minced garlic, chopped hot pepper, cilantro, and salt.
3. Gradually add water, stirring continuously, until you achieve a thick, smooth batter.
4. Heat vegetable oil in a deep pan over medium-high heat for frying.
5. Drop spoonfuls of the batter into the hot oil, frying until golden brown and crispy. Drain on paper towels.

Mutton Filling:

1. In a pan, heat vegetable oil over medium heat. Add chopped onions and minced garlic, sauté until softened.

2. Add shredded mutton to the pan and stir in ground cumin, curry powder, turmeric, salt, and pepper.

3. Cook the mutton mixture until well combined and heated through.

Assembling:

1. Make a small hole in each pholourie and stuff it with a spoonful of the mutton filling.

2. Serve the Mutton Pholourie hot as a delicious and flavorful appetizer or snack.

SOUPS AND STEWS

Guyanese Garlic Pork Soup

Servings: Serves 6

Time: 2 hours

Ingredients:

For the Garlic Pork:

- 1 lb pork belly, cut into small cubes
- 10 cloves garlic, minced
- 2 tablespoons soy sauce
- 1 tablespoon oyster sauce
- 1 tablespoon brown sugar
- 1 teaspoon Chinese five-spice powder
- 1 teaspoon ground black pepper

- **2 tablespoons vegetable oil**

For the Soup:

- **6 cups chicken broth**
- **2 cups water**
- **2 cups pumpkin, peeled and diced**
- **2 cups carrots, peeled and sliced**
- **1 cup cassava, peeled and diced**
- **1 cup cabbage, shredded**
- **Salt and pepper, to taste**
- **Chopped green onions, for garnish**
- **Cooked white rice, for serving**

Directions:

Garlic Pork:

1. **In a bowl, combine minced garlic, soy sauce, oyster sauce, brown sugar, Chinese five-spice powder, and ground black pepper to create a marinade.**
2. **Toss the pork cubes in the marinade until well coated. Let it marinate for at least 30 minutes.**
3. **In a large pot, heat vegetable oil over medium-high heat. Add the marinated pork and cook until browned on all sides.**
4. **Remove the garlic pork from the pot and set it aside.**

Soup:

1. In the same pot, add chicken broth and water. Bring to a boil.
2. Add diced pumpkin, sliced carrots, diced cassava, and shredded cabbage to the boiling broth.
3. Reduce the heat to a simmer and add the cooked garlic pork back into the pot.
4. Simmer the soup for about 30-40 minutes or until the vegetables are tender.
5. Season with salt and pepper to taste.

Metemgee (Mixed Meat Stew with Ground Provisions)

Servings: Serves 8

Time: 2.5 hours

Ingredients:

For the Stew:

- 1 lb beef, cubed
- 1 lb pork, cubed
- 1 lb chicken, cut into pieces
- 1 lb salted pigtail, soaked and cut into chunks
- 1 large onion, chopped
- 4 cloves garlic, minced
- 2 tablespoons vegetable oil
- 2 tablespoons green seasoning (blend of cilantro, green onions, thyme, and other herbs)
- 1 tablespoon curry powder
- 1 teaspoon ground turmeric
- Salt and pepper, to taste
- 4 cups water or beef/chicken broth

For the Ground Provisions:

- 2 large sweet potatoes, peeled and diced
- 2 yams, peeled and diced

- 2 eddoes, peeled and diced
- 2 dasheen, peeled and diced
- 2 plantains, peeled and sliced
- 2 cassava, peeled and diced

Directions:

Stew:

1. In a large pot, heat vegetable oil over medium-high heat. Add chopped onions and minced garlic, sauté until softened.
2. Add the beef, pork, chicken, and salted pigtail to the pot. Brown the meat on all sides.
3. Stir in green seasoning, curry powder, ground turmeric, salt, and pepper. Cook for an additional 5 minutes.
4. Pour in water or broth, bring to a boil, then reduce heat and simmer for 1.5 hours or until the meats are tender.

Ground Provisions:

1. In a separate pot, bring water to a boil. Add diced sweet potatoes, yams, eddoes, dasheen, plantains, and cassava.
2. Boil the ground provisions until they are fork-tender, about 15-20 minutes.

Assembling:

1. When the meat stew is tender, combine it with the boiled ground provisions in a large serving dish.
2. Mix well to allow the flavors to meld.

Black-Eyed Peas and Spinach Cook-up Rice

Servings: Serves 6

Time: 1.5 hours

Ingredients:

- 2 cups white rice
- 1 cup dried black-eyed peas, soaked overnight
- 1 lb spinach, washed and chopped
- 1 onion, finely chopped
- 3 cloves garlic, minced
- 1 red bell pepper, diced
- 1 green bell pepper, diced
- 1 can (14 oz) coconut milk
- 2 tablespoons vegetable oil
- 1 tablespoon green seasoning (blend of cilantro, green onions, thyme, and other herbs)
- 1 teaspoon ground cumin
- 1 teaspoon ground coriander
- Salt and pepper, to taste
- 4 cups water or vegetable broth

Directions:

1. In a large pot, heat vegetable oil over medium-high heat. Add chopped onions and minced garlic, sauté until softened.

2. Add diced red and green bell peppers to the pot, cook for a few minutes until they start to soften.

3. Stir in soaked black-eyed peas, rice, green seasoning, ground cumin, ground coriander, salt, and pepper. Cook for an additional 5 minutes.

4. Pour in coconut milk and water or vegetable broth. Bring the mixture to a boil.

5. Once boiling, reduce the heat to low, cover the pot, and let it simmer for 25-30 minutes or until the rice and black-eyed peas are cooked and the liquid is absorbed.

6. Add chopped spinach to the pot during the last 5 minutes of cooking, stirring to combine and allowing the spinach to wilt.

Fish Broth with Okra

Servings: Serves 4

Time: 1.5 hours

Ingredients:

- 1 lb white fish fillets (snapper or grouper), cut into chunks
- 1 cup okra, sliced
- 1 onion, finely chopped
- 2 cloves garlic, minced
- 1 bell pepper, diced
- 2 tomatoes, chopped
- 1 cup pumpkin, peeled and diced
- 1 cup yams, peeled and diced
- 1 cup cassava, peeled and diced
- 1 cup carrots, peeled and sliced
- 1 hot pepper, whole (optional, for extra heat)
- 1 sprig thyme
- 2 tablespoons vegetable oil
- 6 cups fish or vegetable broth
- Salt and pepper, to taste
- Lime wedges, for serving

Directions:

1. In a large pot, heat vegetable oil over medium-high heat. Add chopped onions and minced garlic, sauté until softened.

2. Add diced bell peppers and tomatoes to the pot, cook for a few minutes until they start to soften.

3. Stir in pumpkin, yams, cassava, carrots, and okra. Cook for an additional 5 minutes.

4. Pour in fish or vegetable broth, add the whole hot pepper (if using), and bring the mixture to a boil.

5. Once boiling, reduce the heat to low, add fish chunks, and simmer for 20-25 minutes or until the vegetables are tender and the fish is cooked through.

6. Season with salt and pepper to taste. Add thyme sprig during the last few minutes of cooking.

7. Remove the hot pepper and thyme sprig before serving.

Pepperpot (Beef and Cassava Stew)

Servings: Serves 6

Time: 3 hours

Ingredients:

- 2 lbs beef, cut into chunks
- 1 lb cassava, peeled and cut into chunks
- 1 onion, finely chopped
- 4 cloves garlic, minced
- 1 cinnamon stick
- 4 cloves
- 2 bay leaves
- 1 tablespoon vegetable oil
- 1 cup cassareep (cassava syrup)
- 1 hot pepper, whole
- Salt, to taste
- Water, as needed

Directions:

1. In a large pot, heat vegetable oil over medium-high heat. Add chopped onions and minced garlic, sauté until softened.
2. Add beef chunks to the pot and brown them on all sides.

3. Pour in enough water to cover the beef, add cinnamon stick, cloves, bay leaves, and the whole hot pepper. Bring the mixture to a boil.

4. Once boiling, reduce the heat to low, cover the pot, and let it simmer for about 2 hours or until the beef is tender.

5. Add cassava chunks to the pot and continue simmering until the cassava is cooked through and tender.

6. Stir in cassareep, ensuring it is well combined with the broth.

7. Season with salt to taste. Continue simmering for an additional 30 minutes to allow the flavors to meld.

8. Remove the cinnamon stick, cloves, bay leaves, and hot pepper before serving.

Pumpkin and Lentil Soup

Servings: Serves 6

Time: 1 hour

Ingredients:

- 1 lb pumpkin, peeled and diced
- 1 cup red lentils, rinsed
- 1 onion, chopped
- 2 carrots, peeled and sliced
- 2 celery stalks, chopped
- 3 cloves garlic, minced
- 1 teaspoon ground cumin
- 1 teaspoon ground coriander
- 1/2 teaspoon turmeric powder
- 6 cups vegetable broth
- 1 bay leaf
- Salt and pepper, to taste
- 2 tablespoons olive oil
- Fresh cilantro or parsley, for garnish (optional)

Directions:

1. In a large pot, heat olive oil over medium heat. Add chopped onions and minced garlic, sauté until softened.

2. Add diced pumpkin, sliced carrots, and chopped celery to the pot. Cook for a few minutes until the vegetables start to soften.

3. Stir in ground cumin, ground coriander, and turmeric powder. Cook for an additional 2 minutes.

4. Add red lentils, vegetable broth, and bay leaf to the pot. Bring the mixture to a boil.

5. Once boiling, reduce the heat to low, cover the pot, and simmer for about 30-40 minutes or until the lentils and vegetables are tender.

6. Remove the bay leaf from the pot and discard.

7. Using an immersion blender, blend the soup until smooth. Alternatively, transfer the soup in batches to a blender, blend, and return to the pot.

8. Season the soup with salt and pepper to taste.

9. Serve the Pumpkin and Lentil Soup hot, garnished with fresh cilantro or parsley if desired.

Chicken Cook-up Rice

Servings: Serves 6

Time: 1.5 hours

Ingredients:

- 2 cups parboiled rice
- 1 lb chicken pieces (thighs or drumsticks)
- 1 cup black-eyed peas, soaked overnight
- 1 onion, finely chopped
- 3 cloves garlic, minced
- 1 bell pepper, diced
- 1 tomato, chopped
- 1 cup coconut milk
- 4 cups chicken broth
- 1 sprig thyme
- 2 tablespoons vegetable oil
- 1 teaspoon ground allspice
- 1 teaspoon ground turmeric
- Salt and pepper, to taste
- Green onions, chopped, for garnish

Directions:

1. In a large pot, heat vegetable oil over medium-high heat. Add chopped onions and minced garlic, sauté until softened.

2. Add chicken pieces to the pot and brown them on all sides.

3. Stir in diced bell pepper and chopped tomato. Cook for a few minutes until they start to soften.

4. Add soaked black-eyed peas, parboiled rice, ground allspice, ground turmeric, and thyme sprig to the pot. Mix well to coat the rice and peas with the spices.

5. Pour in coconut milk and chicken broth. Bring the mixture to a boil.

6. Once boiling, reduce the heat to low, cover the pot, and let it simmer for about 30-40 minutes or until the rice is cooked, and the liquid is absorbed.

7. Season the Chicken Cook-up Rice with salt and pepper to taste.

8. Serve the dish hot, garnished with chopped green onions.

Cabbage and Saltfish Soup

Servings: Serves 4

Time: 1 hour

Ingredients:

- 1 cup salted cod (saltfish), soaked and flaked
- 4 cups cabbage, shredded
- 1 onion, finely chopped
- 2 carrots, peeled and sliced
- 2 potatoes, peeled and diced
- 2 cloves garlic, minced
- 1 scallion, chopped
- 1 sprig thyme
- 1 can (14 oz) coconut milk
- 6 cups water or fish broth
- 2 tablespoons vegetable oil
- 1 teaspoon ground black pepper
- 1 teaspoon paprika
- Salt, to taste
- Lime wedges, for serving

Directions:

1. In a large pot, heat vegetable oil over medium-high heat. Add chopped onions and minced garlic, sauté until softened.

2. Add flaked saltfish to the pot and stir to combine with the onions and garlic. Cook for a few minutes.

3. Pour in coconut milk and water or fish broth. Bring the mixture to a boil.

4. Once boiling, reduce the heat to low, add shredded cabbage, sliced carrots, diced potatoes, scallion, thyme sprig, ground black pepper, paprika, and salt to taste. Stir well.

5. Cover the pot and let the soup simmer for about 30-40 minutes or until the vegetables are tender.

6. Remove the thyme sprig before serving.

Oxtail Stew

Servings: Serves 4

Time: 3 hours

Ingredients:

- 2 lbs oxtail, cut into pieces
- 1 onion, finely chopped
- 4 cloves garlic, minced
- 2 carrots, peeled and sliced
- 2 potatoes, peeled and diced
- 1 cup red wine (optional)
- 4 cups beef broth
- 1 can (14 oz) diced tomatoes
- 2 bay leaves
- 1 sprig thyme
- 2 tablespoons tomato paste
- 2 tablespoons vegetable oil
- 1 cup all-purpose flour (for dredging)
- Salt and pepper, to taste
- Chopped fresh parsley, for garnish (optional)

Directions:

1. In a bowl, season oxtail pieces with salt and pepper. Dredge each piece in flour, shaking off any excess.

2. In a large pot, heat vegetable oil over medium-high heat. Add oxtail pieces and brown them on all sides. Remove and set aside.

3. In the same pot, add chopped onions and minced garlic. Sauté until softened.

4. Pour in red wine (if using) to deglaze the pot, scraping up any browned bits from the bottom.

5. Add browned oxtail back to the pot. Stir in beef broth, diced tomatoes, bay leaves, thyme sprig, and tomato paste. Bring to a boil.

6. Once boiling, reduce the heat to low, cover the pot, and let it simmer for about 2.5-3 hours or until the oxtail is tender.

7. Add sliced carrots and diced potatoes to the pot during the last 30 minutes of cooking.

8. Adjust seasoning with salt and pepper to taste.

9. Remove bay leaves and thyme sprig before serving.

Pumpkin and Shrimp Bisque

Servings: Serves 4

Time: 1.5 hours

Ingredients:

- 1 lb shrimp, peeled and deveined, shells reserved
- 2 cups pumpkin, peeled and diced
- 1 onion, finely chopped
- 2 carrots, peeled and sliced
- 2 celery stalks, chopped
- 3 cloves garlic, minced
- 1/2 cup dry white wine (optional)
- 4 cups vegetable or seafood broth
- 1 cup canned pumpkin puree
- 1 cup coconut milk
- 2 tablespoons olive oil
- 1 teaspoon ground cumin
- 1/2 teaspoon ground nutmeg
- Salt and pepper, to taste

Directions:

1. In a large pot, heat olive oil over medium-high heat. Add chopped onions, sliced carrots, chopped celery, and minced garlic. Sauté until vegetables are softened.

2. Add shrimp shells to the pot and cook for a few minutes to release flavor.

3. Pour in dry white wine (if using) to deglaze the pot, scraping up any browned bits from the bottom.

4. Add diced pumpkin and vegetable or seafood broth to the pot. Bring to a boil, then reduce the heat to low and simmer for about 20-25 minutes or until the pumpkin is tender.

5. Remove the shrimp shells from the pot, leaving the broth and vegetables.

6. Using an immersion blender, blend the mixture until smooth. Alternatively, transfer the soup in batches to a blender, blend, and return to the pot.

7. Stir in canned pumpkin puree, coconut milk, ground cumin, ground nutmeg, salt, and pepper. Simmer for an additional 10 minutes.

8. Add peeled and deveined shrimp to the pot and cook for 5-7 minutes or until the shrimp are pink and cooked through.

9. Adjust seasoning if necessary.

MAIN DISHES - VEGETARIAN

Cook-up Rice with Vegetables

Servings: Serves 4

Time: 1.5 hours

Ingredients:

- **2 cups parboiled rice**
- **1 cup black-eyed peas, soaked overnight**
- **1 cup sliced okra**
- **1 cup pumpkin, peeled and diced**
- **1 cup yams, peeled and diced**
- **1 cup green beans, chopped**
- **1 onion, finely chopped**
- **3 cloves garlic, minced**

- 1 bell pepper, diced
- 1 cup coconut milk
- 4 cups vegetable broth
- 2 tablespoons vegetable oil
- 1 teaspoon ground turmeric
- 1 teaspoon ground cumin
- Salt and pepper, to taste
- Fresh cilantro, chopped, for garnish (optional)

Directions:

1. In a large pot, heat vegetable oil over medium-high heat. Add chopped onions and minced garlic, sauté until softened.
2. Add sliced okra, diced pumpkin, diced yams, chopped green beans, and diced bell pepper to the pot. Cook for a few minutes until the vegetables start to soften.
3. Stir in ground turmeric and ground cumin, coating the vegetables with the spices.
4. Add soaked black-eyed peas, parboiled rice, coconut milk, and vegetable broth to the pot. Bring the mixture to a boil.
5. Once boiling, reduce the heat to low, cover the pot, and let it simmer for about 30-40 minutes or until the rice is cooked and the liquid is absorbed.
6. Season the Cook-up Rice with salt and pepper to taste.

7. **Garnish with chopped fresh cilantro if desired.**

Bhaji and Rice (Spinach and Rice)

Servings: Serves 4

Time: 30 minutes

Ingredients:

- 2 cups fresh spinach, washed and chopped
- 1 cup basmati rice
- 1 onion, finely chopped
- 2 cloves garlic, minced
- 1 tomato, chopped
- 1 green chili, finely chopped (adjust to taste)
- 1 teaspoon cumin seeds
- 1 teaspoon ground coriander
- 1/2 teaspoon turmeric powder
- 2 tablespoons vegetable oil
- Salt, to taste
- Fresh cilantro, chopped, for garnish (optional)

Directions:

1. Rinse the basmati rice under cold water until the water runs clear. Cook the rice according to package instructions.

2. In a large pan, heat vegetable oil over medium-high heat. Add cumin seeds and let them sizzle for a few seconds.

3. Add chopped onions and minced garlic to the pan. Sauté until the onions become translucent.

4. Stir in ground coriander and turmeric powder, coating the onions and garlic with the spices.

5. Add chopped tomatoes and green chili to the pan. Cook until the tomatoes are soft.

6. Toss in the fresh spinach and cook until it wilts down, stirring occasionally.

7. Season the mixture with salt to taste. Cook for an additional 2-3 minutes until the spinach is tender.

8. Serve the Bhaji hot over a bed of cooked basmati rice.

9. Garnish with fresh cilantro if desired.

Baigan Choka (Roasted Eggplant Mash)

Servings: Serves 4

Time: 30 minutes

Ingredients:

- 2 large eggplants
- 1 onion, finely chopped
- 2 cloves garlic, minced
- 1 hot pepper, finely chopped (adjust to taste)
- 2 tablespoons chopped fresh cilantro
- 1 tablespoon olive oil
- Salt and pepper, to taste
- Lime wedges, for serving

Directions:

1. Preheat your oven's broiler. Place the whole eggplants on a baking sheet.
2. Broil the eggplants, turning occasionally, until the skin is charred and the flesh is soft. This may take about 15-20 minutes.
3. Remove the eggplants from the oven and let them cool slightly.
4. Peel off the charred skin from the eggplants and place the flesh in a bowl.

5. Mash the roasted eggplant flesh using a fork or potato masher until it reaches a coarse consistency.

6. In a separate pan, heat olive oil over medium heat. Add chopped onions and minced garlic. Sauté until the onions are translucent.

7. Add the chopped hot pepper to the pan and cook for an additional minute.

8. Mix the sautéed onion, garlic, and hot pepper into the mashed eggplant.

9. Season the Baigan Choka with salt and pepper to taste. Add chopped fresh cilantro and mix well.

10. Serve the Baigan Choka warm, accompanied by lime wedges on the side.

Dhal and Rice with Curry Potatoes

Servings: Serves 4

Time: 45 minutes

Ingredients:

For the Dhal:

- 1 cup yellow split peas (dhal), rinsed
- 4 cups water
- 1 onion, finely chopped
- 3 cloves garlic, minced
- 1 teaspoon ground turmeric
- 1/2 teaspoon ground cumin
- Salt, to taste

For the Rice:

- 1 cup basmati rice
- 2 cups water
- Salt, to taste

For the Curry Potatoes:

- 4 potatoes, peeled and diced
- 1 onion, finely chopped
- 2 tomatoes, chopped
- 2 tablespoons curry powder

- 1 teaspoon ground cumin
- 1 teaspoon ground coriander
- 1/2 teaspoon chili powder (adjust to taste)
- 2 tablespoons vegetable oil
- Salt, to taste

Directions:

For the Dhal:

1. In a large pot, combine yellow split peas, water, chopped onions, minced garlic, ground turmeric, ground cumin, and salt.
2. Bring the mixture to a boil, then reduce the heat to low. Simmer, partially covered, for about 30-40 minutes or until the split peas are soft and the dhal has thickened.

For the Rice:

1. Rinse the basmati rice under cold water until the water runs clear.
2. In a separate pot, combine the rice, water, and salt. Cook the rice according to package instructions.

For the Curry Potatoes:

1. In a pan, heat vegetable oil over medium heat. Add chopped onions and cook until translucent.

2. Stir in curry powder, ground cumin, ground coriander, and chili powder. Cook for an additional 2 minutes.

3. Add diced potatoes and chopped tomatoes to the pan. Mix well to coat the potatoes with the curry mixture.

4. Cover the pan and let the potatoes cook for about 15-20 minutes or until they are tender.

5. Season the curry potatoes with salt to taste.

Channa and Aloo (Chickpeas and Potatoes)

Servings: Serves 4

Time: 45 minutes

Ingredients:

- 2 cups cooked chickpeas (canned or soaked and boiled)
- 2 potatoes, peeled and diced
- 1 onion, finely chopped
- 2 tomatoes, chopped
- 3 cloves garlic, minced
- 1-inch piece ginger, grated
- 1 green chili, finely chopped (adjust to taste)
- 2 tablespoons curry powder
- 1 teaspoon ground cumin
- 1 teaspoon ground coriander
- 1/2 teaspoon turmeric powder
- 2 tablespoons vegetable oil
- Salt and pepper, to taste
- Fresh cilantro, chopped, for garnish (optional)

Directions:

1. In a large pan, heat vegetable oil over medium heat. Add chopped onions and cook until translucent.

2. Stir in minced garlic, grated ginger, and chopped green chili. Cook for an additional 2 minutes.

3. Add curry powder, ground cumin, ground coriander, and turmeric powder to the pan. Mix well to create a fragrant spice blend.

4. Add diced potatoes to the pan and coat them with the spice mixture.

5. Pour in a little water if needed, cover the pan, and let the potatoes cook for about 15 minutes or until they are slightly tender.

6. Stir in chopped tomatoes and cooked chickpeas. Mix well and let the mixture simmer for an additional 10-15 minutes, allowing the flavors to meld.

7. Season the Channa and Aloo with salt and pepper to taste.

8. Garnish with chopped fresh cilantro if desired.

9. Serve the Channa and Aloo hot, over a bed of rice or with your favorite flatbread.

Saheena (Spinach and Split Pea Fritters)

Servings: Makes approximately 15 fritters

Time: 1.5 hours (including soaking time)

Ingredients:

- 1 cup split yellow peas, soaked overnight
- 2 cups fresh spinach, washed and chopped
- 1 onion, finely chopped
- 2 cloves garlic, minced
- 1 hot pepper, finely chopped (adjust to taste)
- 1 teaspoon ground cumin
- 1 teaspoon ground coriander
- 1/2 teaspoon turmeric powder
- 1 cup chopped cilantro
- Salt and pepper, to taste
- Oil for frying

Directions:

1. Rinse the soaked split yellow peas under cold water and drain.

2. In a blender or food processor, combine the soaked split yellow peas, chopped spinach, chopped onion, minced garlic, chopped hot pepper, ground cumin, ground

coriander, and turmeric powder. Blend until you get a coarse, thick paste.

3. Transfer the mixture to a bowl and add chopped cilantro. Mix well.

4. Heat oil in a deep frying pan over medium heat.

5. Using a spoon or your hands, take portions of the mixture and shape them into small fritters.

6. Carefully place the fritters into the hot oil and fry until they are golden brown and crispy. Fry in batches to avoid overcrowding the pan.

7. Remove the fritters with a slotted spoon and place them on a plate lined with paper towels to absorb excess oil.

8. Sprinkle salt and pepper over the hot fritters for added flavor.

Aloo Choka (Mashed Potatoes with Spices)

Servings: Serves 4

Time: 30 minutes

Ingredients:

- 4 large potatoes, peeled and diced
- 1 onion, finely chopped
- 3 cloves garlic, minced
- 1 hot pepper, finely chopped (adjust to taste)
- 1 teaspoon ground cumin
- 1 teaspoon ground coriander
- 1/2 teaspoon turmeric powder
- 2 tablespoons vegetable oil
- Salt and pepper, to taste
- Fresh cilantro, chopped, for garnish (optional)

Directions:

1. Boil the diced potatoes in a pot of salted water until they are fork-tender. Drain and set aside.
2. In a pan, heat vegetable oil over medium heat. Add chopped onions and cook until they are translucent.
3. Stir in minced garlic and chopped hot pepper. Cook for an additional 2 minutes.

4. Add ground cumin, ground coriander, and turmeric powder to the pan. Mix well to create a fragrant spice mixture.

5. Add the boiled potatoes to the pan and mash them with a potato masher or fork, incorporating the spices and seasonings.

6. Season the Aloo Choka with salt and pepper to taste. Continue to mash until you achieve your desired consistency.

7. Garnish with chopped fresh cilantro if desired.

Dhal and Bora (Lentils with Yardlong Beans)

Servings: Serves 4

Time: 45 minutes

Ingredients:

- 1 cup red lentils (masoor dal), rinsed
- 2 cups yardlong beans (bora), trimmed and cut into 1-inch pieces
- 1 onion, finely chopped
- 3 cloves garlic, minced
- 1 hot pepper, finely chopped (adjust to taste)
- 1 teaspoon ground turmeric
- 1 teaspoon ground cumin
- 1 teaspoon ground coriander
- 2 tablespoons vegetable oil
- Salt and pepper, to taste
- Fresh cilantro, chopped, for garnish (optional)

Directions:

1. In a large pot, combine red lentils, chopped onions, minced garlic, chopped hot pepper, ground turmeric, ground cumin, and ground coriander.

2. Add enough water to cover the ingredients and bring the mixture to a boil.

3. Once boiling, reduce the heat to low and let it simmer, partially covered, for about 20-25 minutes or until the lentils are soft and cooked through.

4. In a separate pan, heat vegetable oil over medium heat. Add yardlong beans and sauté for 5-7 minutes until they are slightly tender.

5. Add the sautéed yardlong beans to the pot of simmering lentils. Mix well and continue to simmer for an additional 10-15 minutes.

6. Season the Dhal and Bora with salt and pepper to taste. Adjust the consistency by adding more water if needed.

7. Garnish with chopped fresh cilantro if desired.

Curried Jackfruit

Servings: Serves 4

Time: 45 minutes

Ingredients:

- 2 cans (20 oz each) young green jackfruit, drained and rinsed
- 1 onion, finely chopped
- 3 cloves garlic, minced
- 1-inch piece ginger, grated
- 1 tomato, chopped
- 1 green chili, finely chopped (adjust to taste)
- 2 tablespoons curry powder
- 1 teaspoon ground cumin
- 1 teaspoon ground coriander
- 1/2 teaspoon turmeric powder
- 1 can (14 oz) coconut milk
- 2 tablespoons vegetable oil
- Salt and pepper, to taste
- Fresh cilantro, chopped, for garnish (optional)

Directions:

1. Rinse the young green jackfruit under cold water, draining away the brine. Cut the jackfruit into bite-sized pieces.

2. In a pan, heat vegetable oil over medium heat. Add chopped onions and cook until they are translucent.

3. Stir in minced garlic, grated ginger, and chopped green chili. Cook for an additional 2 minutes.

4. Add curry powder, ground cumin, ground coriander, and turmeric powder to the pan. Mix well to create a fragrant spice blend.

5. Add chopped tomatoes to the pan and cook until they are soft and incorporated into the spice mixture.

6. Add the young green jackfruit pieces to the pan, coating them with the spice mixture.

7. Pour in the coconut milk and bring the mixture to a gentle simmer. Let it simmer for about 20-25 minutes or until the jackfruit is tender and infused with the flavors.

8. Season the Curried Jackfruit with salt and pepper to taste.

9. Garnish with chopped fresh cilantro if desired.

Boulanger and Smoked Herring

Servings: Serves 4

Time: 1.5 hours

Ingredients:

For the Boulanger:

- 4 medium-sized boulanger (Caribbean eggplant), sliced
- 1 onion, thinly sliced
- 2 tomatoes, thinly sliced
- 2 bell peppers (red and green), thinly sliced
- 3 cloves garlic, minced
- 2 sprigs thyme
- 2 tablespoons vegetable oil
- Salt and pepper, to taste

For the Smoked Herring:

- 1 lb smoked herring, boneless and flaked
- 1 onion, finely chopped
- 1 tomato, chopped
- 2 cloves garlic, minced
- 1 hot pepper, finely chopped (adjust to taste)
- 2 tablespoons vegetable oil
- Fresh cilantro or parsley, chopped, for garnish (optional)

Directions:

For the Boulanger:

1. Preheat the oven to 375°F (190°C).
2. In a pan, heat vegetable oil over medium heat. Add minced garlic and sliced onions, sauté until the onions are translucent.
3. Layer the sliced boulanger, tomatoes, bell peppers, sautéed onions and garlic, and thyme sprigs in a baking dish. Repeat the layers until all ingredients are used, finishing with a layer of tomatoes on top.
4. Drizzle a little more vegetable oil over the top layer, and season with salt and pepper.
5. Cover the baking dish with foil and bake for 45 minutes. Remove the foil and bake for an additional 15 minutes or until the vegetables are tender.

For the Smoked Herring:

1. In a pan, heat vegetable oil over medium heat. Add chopped onions and minced garlic, sauté until the onions are translucent.
2. Stir in chopped tomatoes and hot pepper. Cook for an additional 2 minutes.

3. Add flaked smoked herring to the pan, mixing well with the vegetables. Cook for about 10 minutes, stirring occasionally.

4. Adjust seasoning if needed.

MAIN DISHES - MEAT AND SEAFOOD

Curry Chicken with Roti

Servings: Serves 4

Time: 1.5 hours

Ingredients:

For the Curry Chicken:

- 2 lbs chicken pieces (preferably with bone-in and skin-on)
- 1 onion, finely chopped
- 3 cloves garlic, minced
- 1-inch piece ginger, grated
- 2 tomatoes, chopped

- 2 potatoes, peeled and diced
- 1 cup coconut milk
- 2 tablespoons curry powder
- 1 teaspoon ground cumin
- 1 teaspoon ground coriander
- 1/2 teaspoon turmeric powder
- 1 hot pepper, finely chopped (adjust to taste)
- 2 tablespoons vegetable oil
- Salt and pepper, to taste
- Fresh cilantro, chopped, for garnish (optional)

For the Roti:

- 2 cups all-purpose flour
- 1/2 teaspoon baking powder
- 1/2 teaspoon salt
- 3/4 cup warm water
- 2 tablespoons vegetable oil

Directions:

For the Curry Chicken:

1. In a large pot, heat vegetable oil over medium heat. Add chopped onions, minced garlic, and grated ginger. Sauté until the onions are translucent.

2. Add curry powder, ground cumin, ground coriander, and turmeric powder to the pot. Mix well to create a fragrant spice blend.

3. Add chicken pieces to the pot, coating them with the spice mixture. Cook until the chicken is browned on all sides.

4. Stir in chopped tomatoes and hot pepper. Cook for a few minutes until the tomatoes are soft.

5. Add diced potatoes and coconut milk to the pot. Mix well and bring the mixture to a simmer.

6. Reduce the heat to low, cover the pot, and let it simmer for about 45-60 minutes or until the chicken is cooked through and the potatoes are tender.

7. Season the Curry Chicken with salt and pepper to taste.

8. Garnish with chopped fresh cilantro if desired.

For the Roti:

1. In a bowl, mix the all-purpose flour, baking powder, and salt.

2. Gradually add warm water to the flour mixture, kneading to form a soft and smooth dough.

3. Divide the dough into golf ball-sized portions. Roll each portion into a ball.

4. Flatten each ball into a thin round disc using a rolling pin.

5. Heat a griddle or flat pan over medium heat. Place the flattened dough on the hot surface and cook until bubbles form, then flip and cook the other side.
6. Brush each side of the roti with vegetable oil during the cooking process.
7. Continue this process until all the roti are cooked.

Garlic Butter Shrimp

Servings: Serves 4

Time: 15 minutes

Ingredients:

- 1 lb large shrimp, peeled and deveined
- 4 tablespoons unsalted butter
- 4 cloves garlic, minced
- 1 teaspoon paprika
- 1/2 teaspoon red pepper flakes (adjust to taste)
- Salt and pepper, to taste
- 2 tablespoons fresh parsley, chopped
- 1 tablespoon lemon juice

Directions:

1. In a large skillet, melt the butter over medium heat.
2. Add minced garlic to the melted butter and sauté for 1-2 minutes until fragrant.
3. Add the shrimp to the skillet, spreading them in a single layer.
4. Sprinkle paprika and red pepper flakes over the shrimp. Season with salt and pepper to taste.
5. Cook the shrimp for 2-3 minutes on one side until they start to turn pink.

6. Flip the shrimp and cook for an additional 2-3 minutes on the other side until they are opaque and cooked through.

7. Stir in chopped fresh parsley and lemon juice, mixing well to coat the shrimp evenly.

8. Remove the skillet from heat.

Peppered Beef

Servings: Serves 4

Time: 1.5 hours

Ingredients:

- **1.5 lbs beef sirloin or flank steak, thinly sliced**
- **2 onions, thinly sliced**
- **4 bell peppers (assorted colors), thinly sliced**
- **3 cloves garlic, minced**
- **1 tablespoon ginger, grated**
- **2 tomatoes, chopped**
- **2 tablespoons soy sauce**
- **2 tablespoons oyster sauce**
- **2 tablespoons vegetable oil**
- **1 teaspoon black pepper**
- **1 teaspoon crushed red pepper flakes (adjust to taste)**
- **Salt, to taste**
- **Fresh cilantro, chopped, for garnish (optional)**

Directions:

1. **In a bowl, marinate the thinly sliced beef with soy sauce, oyster sauce, black pepper, and a pinch of salt. Let it marinate for at least 30 minutes.**

2. In a large wok or skillet, heat vegetable oil over high heat.

3. Add minced garlic and grated ginger to the hot oil. Sauté for a minute until fragrant.

4. Add the marinated beef slices to the wok. Stir-fry for 2-3 minutes until the beef is browned and cooked through. Remove the beef from the wok and set it aside.

5. In the same wok, add a bit more oil if needed. Sauté sliced onions and bell peppers until they are slightly tender but still crisp.

6. Stir in chopped tomatoes and continue cooking for another 2-3 minutes until the tomatoes are softened.

7. Return the cooked beef to the wok, tossing everything together to combine. Cook for an additional 2-3 minutes to heat through.

8. Adjust the seasoning with salt and crushed red pepper flakes to taste.

9. Garnish with chopped fresh cilantro if desired.

10. Serve the Peppered Beef hot over steamed rice or with your favorite side.

Fried Bangamary (Fish)

Servings: Serves 4

Time: 30 minutes

Ingredients:

- **4 bangamary fish fillets (or any white fish fillets), cleaned and scaled**
- **1 cup all-purpose flour**
- **1 teaspoon garlic powder**
- **1 teaspoon onion powder**
- **1/2 teaspoon paprika**
- **Salt and pepper, to taste**
- **Vegetable oil, for frying**
- **Lemon wedges, for serving**

Directions:

1. **In a shallow bowl, combine all-purpose flour, garlic powder, onion powder, paprika, salt, and pepper. Mix well to create a seasoned coating for the fish.**
2. **Pat the fish fillets dry with a paper towel to remove excess moisture.**
3. **Heat vegetable oil in a frying pan or skillet over medium-high heat, enough to submerge the fish fillets.**

4. Dredge each fish fillet in the seasoned flour mixture, coating both sides evenly.

5. Carefully place the coated fish fillets in the hot oil, frying for about 3-4 minutes on each side or until they are golden brown and crispy.

6. Use a slotted spoon to remove the fried fish from the oil and place them on a plate lined with paper towels to absorb any excess oil.

7. Repeat the process for the remaining fish fillets.

8. Serve the Fried Bangamary hot, with lemon wedges on the side for a burst of citrus flavor.

Chicken Curry with Pumpkin

Servings: Serves 4

Time: 1.5 hours

Ingredients:

- 2 lbs chicken pieces (preferably with bone-in and skin-on)
- 2 cups pumpkin, peeled and diced
- 1 onion, finely chopped
- 3 cloves garlic, minced
- 1-inch piece ginger, grated
- 2 tomatoes, chopped
- 1 cup coconut milk
- 2 tablespoons curry powder
- 1 teaspoon ground cumin
- 1 teaspoon ground coriander
- 1/2 teaspoon turmeric powder
- 1 hot pepper, finely chopped (adjust to taste)
- 2 tablespoons vegetable oil
- Salt and pepper, to taste
- Fresh cilantro, chopped, for garnish (optional)

Directions:

1. In a large pot, heat vegetable oil over medium heat. Add chopped onions, minced garlic, and grated ginger. Sauté until the onions are translucent.

2. Add curry powder, ground cumin, ground coriander, and turmeric powder to the pot. Mix well to create a fragrant spice blend.

3. Add chicken pieces to the pot, coating them with the spice mixture. Cook until the chicken is browned on all sides.

4. Stir in chopped tomatoes and hot pepper. Cook for a few minutes until the tomatoes are soft.

5. Add diced pumpkin and coconut milk to the pot. Mix well and bring the mixture to a simmer.

6. Reduce the heat to low, cover the pot, and let it simmer for about 45-60 minutes or until the chicken is cooked through, and the pumpkin is tender.

7. Season the Chicken Curry with Pumpkin with salt and pepper to taste.

8. Garnish with chopped fresh cilantro if desired.

Garlic Pork with Cassava

Servings: Serves 4

Time: 2 hours

Ingredients:

For the Garlic Pork:

- 1.5 lbs pork shoulder, cut into bite-sized pieces
- 1 onion, finely chopped
- 6 cloves garlic, minced
- 1-inch piece ginger, grated
- 2 tablespoons soy sauce
- 1 tablespoon oyster sauce
- 1 teaspoon brown sugar
- 1 teaspoon ground black pepper
- 2 tablespoons vegetable oil
- 1 cup water

For the Cassava:

- 2 lbs cassava, peeled and cut into chunks
- Salt, to taste

Directions:

For the Garlic Pork:

1. In a bowl, marinate the pork pieces with soy sauce, oyster sauce, brown sugar, and black pepper. Let it marinate for at least 30 minutes.

2. In a large pot or Dutch oven, heat vegetable oil over medium-high heat. Add chopped onions, minced garlic, and grated ginger. Sauté until the onions are translucent.

3. Add the marinated pork to the pot, stirring to brown the pieces on all sides.

4. Pour in 1 cup of water and bring the mixture to a boil. Reduce the heat to low, cover the pot, and let it simmer for 1.5 to 2 hours or until the pork is tender and the sauce has thickened.

5. Adjust the seasoning if needed.

For the Cassava:

1. In a separate pot, bring water to a boil. Add salt to the boiling water.

2. Add the cassava chunks to the boiling water and cook for about 20-30 minutes or until the cassava is tender when pierced with a fork.

3. Drain the cassava and let it cool slightly.

4. Serve the Garlic Pork with Cassava hot, with the cassava chunks on the side.

Duck Curry

Servings: Serves 4

Time: 2 hours

Ingredients:

- 2 lbs duck, cleaned and cut into pieces
- 1 onion, finely chopped
- 3 cloves garlic, minced
- 1-inch piece ginger, grated
- 2 tomatoes, chopped
- 1 cup coconut milk
- 2 tablespoons curry powder
- 1 teaspoon ground cumin
- 1 teaspoon ground coriander
- 1/2 teaspoon turmeric powder
- 1 hot pepper, finely chopped (adjust to taste)
- 2 tablespoons vegetable oil
- Salt and pepper, to taste
- Fresh cilantro, chopped, for garnish (optional)

Directions:

1. In a large pot, heat vegetable oil over medium heat. Add chopped onions, minced garlic, and grated ginger. Sauté until the onions are translucent.

2. Add curry powder, ground cumin, ground coriander, and turmeric powder to the pot. Mix well to create a fragrant spice blend.

3. Add duck pieces to the pot, coating them with the spice mixture. Cook until the duck is browned on all sides.

4. Stir in chopped tomatoes and hot pepper. Cook for a few minutes until the tomatoes are soft.

5. Add coconut milk to the pot. Mix well and bring the mixture to a simmer.

6. Reduce the heat to low, cover the pot, and let it simmer for about 1.5 to 2 hours or until the duck is tender.

7. Season the Duck Curry with salt and pepper to taste.

8. Garnish with chopped fresh cilantro if desired.

Masala Salmon

Servings: Serves 4

Time: 30 minutes

Ingredients:

- 4 salmon fillets
- 1 onion, finely chopped
- 3 cloves garlic, minced
- 1-inch piece ginger, grated
- 2 tomatoes, chopped
- 1/2 cup plain yogurt
- 2 tablespoons tomato paste
- 2 teaspoons garam masala
- 1 teaspoon ground cumin
- 1 teaspoon ground coriander
- 1/2 teaspoon turmeric powder
- 1/2 teaspoon chili powder (adjust to taste)
- Salt and pepper, to taste
- 2 tablespoons vegetable oil
- Fresh cilantro, chopped, for garnish (optional)
- Lemon wedges, for serving

Directions:

1. In a bowl, mix together yogurt, tomato paste, garam masala, ground cumin, ground coriander, turmeric powder, chili powder, salt, and pepper to create the marinade.

2. Place the salmon fillets in a shallow dish and coat them with the marinade. Let them marinate for at least 15-20 minutes.

3. In a large pan, heat vegetable oil over medium heat. Add chopped onions and cook until they are translucent.

4. Add minced garlic and grated ginger to the pan. Sauté for an additional 2 minutes until fragrant.

5. Stir in chopped tomatoes and cook until they are soft and incorporated into the mixture.

6. Place the marinated salmon fillets in the pan, spooning some of the marinade over them.

7. Cook the salmon for 4-5 minutes on each side or until they are cooked through and easily flake with a fork.

8. Garnish with chopped fresh cilantro if desired and serve the Masala Salmon hot, with lemon wedges on the side.

Beef Chow Mein

Servings: Serves 4

Time: 30 minutes

Ingredients:

- 8 oz chow mein noodles (or egg noodles)
- 1 lb beef sirloin, thinly sliced
- 2 cups mixed vegetables (such as bell peppers, broccoli, carrots, and snap peas), sliced
- 1 onion, thinly sliced
- 3 cloves garlic, minced
- 1-inch piece ginger, grated
- 1/4 cup soy sauce
- 2 tablespoons oyster sauce
- 1 tablespoon hoisin sauce
- 1 tablespoon cornstarch
- 2 tablespoons vegetable oil
- Salt and pepper, to taste
- Green onions, chopped, for garnish (optional)
- Sesame seeds, for garnish (optional)

Directions:

1. Cook the chow mein noodles according to the package instructions. Drain and set aside.

2. In a bowl, mix soy sauce, oyster sauce, hoisin sauce, and cornstarch to create the sauce. Set aside.

3. Heat vegetable oil in a wok or large skillet over high heat.

4. Add thinly sliced beef to the hot oil, seasoning with salt and pepper. Stir-fry for 2-3 minutes until the beef is browned and cooked through. Remove the beef from the wok and set it aside.

5. In the same wok, add a bit more oil if needed. Sauté sliced onions, minced garlic, and grated ginger until the onions are translucent.

6. Add mixed vegetables to the wok, stir-frying for 3-4 minutes until they are slightly tender but still crisp.

7. Return the cooked beef to the wok, tossing everything together.

8. Pour the prepared sauce over the beef and vegetables, mixing well. Cook for an additional 2-3 minutes until the sauce thickens.

9. Add the cooked chow mein noodles to the wok, tossing to coat them evenly with the beef, vegetables, and sauce.

10. Garnish with chopped green onions and sesame seeds if desired.

Fried Tilapia with Creole Sauce

Servings: Serves 4

Time: 30 minutes

Ingredients:

For the Fried Tilapia:

- **4 tilapia fillets**
- **1 cup all-purpose flour**
- **1 teaspoon garlic powder**
- **1 teaspoon onion powder**
- **1/2 teaspoon paprika**
- **Salt and pepper, to taste**
- **Vegetable oil, for frying**

For the Creole Sauce:

- **1 onion, finely chopped**
- **1 bell pepper (red or green), finely chopped**
- **2 celery stalks, finely chopped**
- **3 cloves garlic, minced**
- **1 can (14 oz) diced tomatoes**
- **1 teaspoon dried thyme**
- **1 teaspoon dried oregano**
- **1/2 teaspoon cayenne pepper (adjust to taste)**
- **Salt and pepper, to taste**

- 2 tablespoons vegetable oil
- Fresh parsley, chopped, for garnish (optional)

Directions:

For the Fried Tilapia:

1. In a shallow bowl, combine all-purpose flour, garlic powder, onion powder, paprika, salt, and pepper. Mix well to create a seasoned coating for the tilapia fillets.
2. Pat the tilapia fillets dry with a paper towel to remove excess moisture.
3. Dredge each tilapia fillet in the seasoned flour mixture, coating both sides evenly.
4. Heat vegetable oil in a frying pan or skillet over medium-high heat.
5. Carefully place the coated tilapia fillets in the hot oil, frying for about 3-4 minutes on each side or until they are golden brown and crispy.
6. Use a slotted spoon to remove the fried tilapia from the oil and place them on a plate lined with paper towels to absorb any excess oil.

For the Creole Sauce:

1. In a separate pan, heat vegetable oil over medium heat. Add chopped onions, bell peppers, and celery. Sauté until the vegetables are softened.

2. Add minced garlic to the pan and cook for an additional 2 minutes until fragrant.

3. Stir in diced tomatoes, dried thyme, dried oregano, cayenne pepper, salt, and pepper. Simmer for 10-15 minutes, allowing the flavors to meld.

4. Adjust seasoning if needed.

5. Serve the Fried Tilapia with Creole Sauce hot, spooning the sauce over the tilapia fillets. Garnish with chopped fresh parsley if desired.

DESSERTS AND SWEETS

Guyanese Black Cake

Servings: Makes 1 cake (about 10-12 servings)

Time: 3-4 hours (including soaking time)

Ingredients:

For the Fruit Mixture:

- 1 lb mixed dried fruits (raisins, currants, prunes, mixed peel)
- 1 cup rum (dark or golden)
- 1 cup cherry brandy
- Zest of 1 lemon
- Zest of 1 orange

For the Cake Batter:

- 1 cup unsalted butter, softened
- 1 cup granulated sugar
- 6 large eggs
- 2 cups all-purpose flour
- 1 teaspoon baking powder
- 1 teaspoon mixed spice (blend of cinnamon, nutmeg, and cloves)
- 1/2 cup browning (burnt sugar)
- 1/2 cup molasses
- 1/4 cup cherry brandy (from soaked fruit mixture)
- 1/4 cup rum (from soaked fruit mixture)
- 1 teaspoon vanilla extract

For Brushing and Soaking:

- 1/4 cup cherry brandy
- 1/4 cup rum

Directions:

Prepare the Fruit Mixture:

1. Combine mixed dried fruits, rum, cherry brandy, lemon zest, and orange zest in a large bowl.
2. Cover the bowl and let the fruit mixture soak for at least 24 hours, preferably for a few days or up to a week.

Make the Cake Batter:

1. Preheat the oven to 325°F (163°C). Grease and line a cake pan with parchment paper.
2. In a large bowl, cream together softened butter and sugar until light and fluffy.
3. Add eggs one at a time, beating well after each addition.
4. In a separate bowl, sift together all-purpose flour, baking powder, and mixed spice.
5. Gradually add the dry ingredients to the creamed mixture, mixing until well combined.
6. Fold in the browning, molasses, cherry brandy, rum, and vanilla extract until the batter is smooth.
7. Add the soaked fruit mixture (including any liquid) to the batter and mix until the fruit is evenly distributed.

Bake the Cake:

1. Pour the batter into the prepared cake pan and smooth the top with a spatula.
2. Bake in the preheated oven for 2.5 to 3 hours or until a toothpick inserted into the center comes out clean.
3. Remove the cake from the oven and let it cool in the pan for 10-15 minutes.
4. Use a skewer to poke holes in the cake, and brush the top with a mixture of cherry brandy and rum.
5. Let the cake cool completely in the pan before transferring it to a wire rack.

Soak the Cake:

1. Once the cake is completely cooled, brush it again with a mixture of cherry brandy and rum.

2. Wrap the cake tightly in plastic wrap and aluminum foil.

3. Allow the cake to mature by letting it rest for at least a week, preferably longer. The longer it sits, the richer the flavors become.

Salara (Coconut Roll)

Servings: Makes 1 roll

Time: 2 hours (including resting time)

Ingredients:

For the Dough:

- 3 cups all-purpose flour
- 1/2 cup granulated sugar
- 1 teaspoon baking powder
- 1/4 teaspoon salt
- 1/2 cup unsalted butter, chilled and cubed
- 1/2 cup coconut milk
- 1 large egg, beaten

For the Filling:

- 2 cups grated coconut (fresh or desiccated)
- 1 cup granulated sugar
- 1 teaspoon ground cinnamon
- 1/4 cup water

For the Glaze:

- 1/2 cup powdered sugar
- 2 tablespoons coconut milk

Directions:

Prepare the Dough:

1. In a large bowl, combine all-purpose flour, sugar, baking powder, and salt.
2. Add chilled and cubed butter to the dry ingredients. Use your fingertips to rub the butter into the flour until the mixture resembles coarse crumbs.
3. Make a well in the center and add coconut milk and beaten egg. Mix until the dough comes together.
4. Turn the dough onto a floured surface and knead for a few minutes until it becomes smooth.
5. Wrap the dough in plastic wrap and refrigerate for at least 30 minutes.

Prepare the Filling:

1. In a saucepan, combine grated coconut, sugar, ground cinnamon, and water.
2. Cook over medium heat, stirring continuously, until the mixture thickens and becomes a cohesive filling.
3. Remove from heat and let it cool.

Assemble the Salara:

1. Preheat the oven to 350°F (175°C). Line a baking sheet with parchment paper.

2. Roll out the chilled dough on a floured surface into a rectangle, about 12x18 inches.

3. Spread the cooled coconut filling evenly over the dough, leaving a small border around the edges.

4. Starting from one long edge, tightly roll the dough into a log.

5. Place the rolled dough seam-side down on the prepared baking sheet.

Bake the Salara:

1. Bake in the preheated oven for 30-35 minutes or until the Salara is golden brown.

2. Remove from the oven and let it cool on the baking sheet.

Prepare the Glaze:

1. In a small bowl, whisk together powdered sugar and coconut milk until you have a smooth glaze.

2. Drizzle the glaze over the cooled Salara.

Chocolate Walnut Fudge

Servings: Makes about 36 pieces

Time: 2 hours (including chilling time)

Ingredients:

- 3 cups semi-sweet chocolate chips
- 1 can (14 oz) sweetened condensed milk
- 1/4 cup unsalted butter
- 1 teaspoon vanilla extract
- 1/2 cup chopped walnuts (optional)
- Pinch of salt

Directions:

1. Line an 8-inch square baking pan with parchment paper, leaving an overhang on two sides for easy removal.
2. In a medium-sized saucepan over low heat, combine chocolate chips, sweetened condensed milk, and butter. Stir continuously until the chocolate and butter are completely melted, and the mixture is smooth.
3. Remove the saucepan from heat and stir in vanilla extract and a pinch of salt.
4. If desired, fold in the chopped walnuts until evenly distributed throughout the fudge mixture.

5. Pour the fudge mixture into the prepared baking pan, spreading it out evenly with a spatula.

6. Refrigerate the fudge for at least 2 hours or until it is firm and set.

7. Once the fudge is completely chilled, use the parchment paper overhangs to lift it out of the pan.

8. Place the block of fudge on a cutting board and use a sharp knife to cut it into small squares.

9. Store the fudge in an airtight container in the refrigerator.

Pine Tart

Servings: Makes about 12 tarts

Time: 1.5 hours (including chilling time)

Ingredients:

For the Tart Crust:

- 2 cups all-purpose flour
- 1 cup unsalted butter, cold and cubed
- 1/2 cup granulated sugar
- 1 large egg
- 1 teaspoon vanilla extract
- Pinch of salt

For the Pine Filling:

- 2 cups pineapple, finely chopped
- 1 cup granulated sugar
- 1/2 cup water
- 1 cinnamon stick
- 1 teaspoon lemon juice

Directions:

Prepare the Tart Crust:

1. In a food processor, combine all-purpose flour, cold cubed butter, granulated sugar, egg, vanilla extract, and a pinch of salt.
2. Pulse the ingredients until the mixture resembles coarse crumbs.
3. Turn the dough out onto a floured surface and knead it just until it comes together. Shape it into a disk, wrap it in plastic wrap, and refrigerate for at least 30 minutes.

Prepare the Pine Filling:

1. In a saucepan, combine chopped pineapple, granulated sugar, water, cinnamon stick, and lemon juice.
2. Cook over medium heat, stirring frequently until the mixture thickens, and the pineapple is soft. This usually takes about 15-20 minutes.
3. Remove the cinnamon stick and let the filling cool.

Assemble the Pine Tarts:

1. Preheat the oven to 350°F (175°C). Grease a muffin tin.
2. Roll out the chilled dough on a floured surface. Cut out circles large enough to line the muffin tin.
3. Press each circle into the muffin cups to form tart shells.
4. Fill each tart shell with the cooled pineapple filling.

Bake the Pine Tarts:

1. Bake in the preheated oven for about 20-25 minutes or until the crust is golden brown.

2. Remove the tarts from the oven and let them cool in the muffin tin for a few minutes before transferring them to a wire rack to cool completely.

Jam Tart

Servings: Makes one 9-inch tart

Time: 1.5 hours (including chilling time)

Ingredients:

For the Tart Crust:

- 1 1/2 cups all-purpose flour
- 1/2 cup unsalted butter, cold and cubed
- 1/4 cup granulated sugar
- 1 large egg yolk
- 2 tablespoons ice water

For the Jam Filling:

- 1 cup fruit jam of your choice (such as raspberry, strawberry, or apricot)

Directions:

Prepare the Tart Crust:

1. In a food processor, combine all-purpose flour, cold cubed butter, granulated sugar, egg yolk, and ice water.
2. Pulse the ingredients until the mixture resembles coarse crumbs.

3. Turn the dough out onto a lightly floured surface. Knead it just until it comes together, shape it into a disk, wrap it in plastic wrap, and refrigerate for at least 30 minutes.

Assemble the Jam Tart:

1. Preheat the oven to 375°F (190°C). Grease a 9-inch tart pan with a removable bottom.
2. Roll out the chilled dough on a floured surface into a circle slightly larger than your tart pan.
3. Gently press the rolled-out dough into the bottom and sides of the tart pan. Trim any excess dough from the edges.
4. Prick the bottom of the tart crust with a fork to prevent it from puffing up during baking.
5. Spread the fruit jam evenly over the tart crust.

Bake the Jam Tart:

1. Bake in the preheated oven for 20-25 minutes or until the crust is golden brown.
2. Remove the tart from the oven and let it cool in the pan for a few minutes before transferring it to a wire rack to cool completely.

Custard Block

Servings: Makes about 16 squares

Time: 2 hours (including chilling time)

Ingredients:

For the Custard Layer:

- **2 cups whole milk**
- **1 cup heavy cream**
- **1 cup granulated sugar**
- **1/2 cup cornstarch**
- **4 large egg yolks**
- **1 teaspoon vanilla extract**

For the Biscuit Layer:

- **2 cups crushed tea biscuits**
- **1/2 cup unsalted butter, melted**

For the Chocolate Ganache Topping:

- **1 cup semi-sweet chocolate chips**
- **1/2 cup heavy cream**

Directions:

Prepare the Custard Layer:

1. In a saucepan, combine whole milk and heavy cream. Heat over medium heat until it just begins to simmer.

2. In a separate bowl, whisk together granulated sugar, cornstarch, and egg yolks until well combined.

3. Slowly pour the hot milk mixture into the egg mixture, whisking continuously to prevent curdling.

4. Return the mixture to the saucepan and cook over medium heat, stirring constantly, until it thickens to a custard consistency.

5. Remove from heat, stir in vanilla extract, and let the custard cool.

Prepare the Biscuit Layer:

1. In a bowl, combine crushed tea biscuits and melted butter. Mix until the crumbs are evenly coated.

2. Press the biscuit mixture into the bottom of a square baking dish to form an even layer.

3. Refrigerate the biscuit layer while the custard cools.

Assemble the Custard Block:

1. Once the custard has cooled, spread it evenly over the chilled biscuit layer.

2. Refrigerate the entire dish to allow the custard to set, preferably for at least 1 hour.

Prepare the Chocolate Ganache Topping:

1. In a heatproof bowl, combine chocolate chips and heavy cream.
2. Microwave the mixture in 30-second intervals, stirring each time, until the chocolate is fully melted and the ganache is smooth.
3. Let the ganache cool slightly before pouring it over the set custard layer.

Finish and Chill:

1. Spread the chocolate ganache evenly over the custard layer.
2. Refrigerate the entire Custard Block for at least 1 more hour to allow the chocolate ganache to set.
3. Cut it into squares before serving.

Mithai (Guyanese Milk Fudge)

Servings: Makes about 24 pieces

Time: 1.5 hours (including cooling time)

Ingredients:

- 2 cups full-fat milk powder
- 1 cup sweetened condensed milk
- 1/2 cup unsalted butter
- 1/2 cup water
- 1/2 cup granulated sugar
- 1/2 teaspoon ground cardamom
- 1/4 cup chopped nuts (such as almonds or pistachios) for garnish (optional)

Directions:

1. In a mixing bowl, combine the milk powder and sweetened condensed milk. Mix well to form a smooth, lump-free mixture. Set aside.
2. In a saucepan, melt the butter over medium heat.
3. Add water and granulated sugar to the melted butter. Stir continuously until the sugar dissolves.
4. Lower the heat and gradually add the milk powder and condensed milk mixture to the saucepan. Stir continuously to avoid lumps.

5. Continue stirring the mixture over medium heat until it thickens and starts to leave the sides of the pan. This process may take around 10-15 minutes.

6. Add ground cardamom to the mixture and continue stirring until it reaches a fudge-like consistency. The mixture should be smooth and glossy.

7. Remove the saucepan from heat and let the mixture cool slightly.

8. Once the mixture is cool enough to handle, grease your hands with a bit of butter and shape the fudge into small bite-sized pieces. You can roll them into rounds or shape them as desired.

9. If using nuts for garnish, press a piece of chopped nut onto the top of each fudge piece.

10. Let the Mithai cool completely before serving.

Cassava Pone

Servings: Makes about 12 squares

Time: 2 hours (including baking time)

Ingredients:

- 4 cups grated cassava
- 1 cup grated coconut
- 1 cup granulated sugar
- 1/2 cup melted butter
- 1 cup coconut milk
- 1 teaspoon vanilla extract
- 1/2 teaspoon ground cinnamon
- 1/2 teaspoon ground nutmeg
- 1/4 teaspoon salt
- 1/2 cup raisins (optional)
- 1/4 cup chopped cashews or almonds (optional)

Directions:

1. Preheat the oven to 350°F (175°C). Grease a baking dish (approximately 9x9 inches) or line it with parchment paper.
2. In a large bowl, combine grated cassava, grated coconut, granulated sugar, melted butter, coconut milk, vanilla

extract, ground cinnamon, ground nutmeg, and salt. Mix well to ensure all ingredients are thoroughly combined.

3. If desired, fold in raisins and chopped nuts into the mixture.

4. Pour the cassava mixture into the prepared baking dish, spreading it out evenly.

5. Bake in the preheated oven for about 1.5 to 2 hours or until the top is golden brown and a toothpick inserted into the center comes out clean.

6. Remove from the oven and let it cool in the baking dish for about 15 minutes.

7. Once slightly cooled, cut the Cassava Pone into squares while it's still in the baking dish.

8. Allow it to cool completely before serving.

Coconut Buns

Servings: Makes about 12 buns

Time: 2.5 hours (including rising and baking time)

Ingredients:

For the Dough:

- 4 cups all-purpose flour
- 1/2 cup granulated sugar
- 1 tablespoon active dry yeast
- 1/2 teaspoon salt
- 1 cup warm milk
- 1/4 cup unsalted butter, melted
- 1 large egg

For the Coconut Filling:

- 2 cups shredded coconut
- 1/2 cup brown sugar
- 1/4 cup unsalted butter, melted

For the Glaze:

- 1/4 cup apricot jam (or any fruit jam)
- 1 tablespoon water

Directions:

Prepare the Dough:

1. In a bowl, combine warm milk and sugar. Sprinkle the active dry yeast over the milk mixture and let it sit for 5-10 minutes until it becomes frothy.
2. In a large mixing bowl, combine flour and salt. Make a well in the center.
3. Pour the activated yeast mixture, melted butter, and beaten egg into the well.
4. Mix the ingredients to form a dough. Knead the dough on a floured surface for about 8-10 minutes until it becomes smooth and elastic.
5. Place the dough in a greased bowl, cover it with a damp cloth, and let it rise in a warm place for about 1-1.5 hours or until it doubles in size.

Prepare the Coconut Filling:

1. In a bowl, mix shredded coconut, brown sugar, and melted butter until well combined.

Assemble the Coconut Buns:

1. Preheat the oven to 375°F (190°C). Grease or line a baking sheet.
2. Punch down the risen dough and turn it out onto a floured surface.

3. Roll out the dough into a rectangle.

4. Spread the coconut filling evenly over the surface of the dough.

5. Roll the dough tightly from one of the longer sides, forming a log.

6. Cut the log into 12 equal pieces.

7. Place the cut pieces on the prepared baking sheet, leaving some space between each bun.

8. Cover the buns with a damp cloth and let them rise for an additional 30 minutes.

Bake the Coconut Buns:

1. Bake in the preheated oven for 15-20 minutes or until the buns are golden brown.

2. While the buns are baking, prepare the glaze by heating apricot jam and water in a small saucepan until it becomes a smooth mixture.

3. Once the buns are out of the oven, brush them with the apricot glaze for a shiny finish.

Salara (Coconut Roll) Ice Cream

Servings: Makes about 1 quart

Time: 4 hours (including freezing time)

Ingredients:

For the Salara Swirl:

- 1 cup grated coconut
- 1/2 cup granulated sugar
- 1/4 cup water
- 1/2 teaspoon ground cinnamon
- 1/4 cup desiccated coconut (for texture)

For the Ice Cream Base:

- 2 cups heavy cream
- 1 cup whole milk
- 1 cup granulated sugar
- 1 teaspoon vanilla extract
- 4 large egg yolks

Directions:

Prepare the Salara Swirl:

1. In a saucepan, combine grated coconut, granulated sugar, water, and ground cinnamon.

2. Cook over medium heat, stirring frequently until the mixture thickens and the coconut is coated with the sugar syrup. This usually takes about 10-15 minutes.

3. Remove from heat and let it cool. Once cooled, stir in desiccated coconut for added texture.

Prepare the Ice Cream Base:

1. In a medium saucepan, heat the heavy cream and whole milk over medium heat until it just begins to simmer. Remove from heat.

2. In a separate bowl, whisk together egg yolks and granulated sugar until the mixture becomes pale and slightly thick.

3. Gradually pour the hot milk mixture into the egg yolk mixture, whisking constantly to avoid curdling.

4. Return the combined mixture to the saucepan and cook over low heat, stirring continuously, until it thickens enough to coat the back of a spoon. Do not let it boil.

5. Remove from heat, stir in vanilla extract, and let the ice cream base cool.

Assemble the Salara Swirl Ice Cream:

1. Once the ice cream base is completely cooled, churn it in an ice cream maker according to the manufacturer's instructions.

2. In the last few minutes of churning, add the Salara swirl mixture, allowing it to evenly distribute throughout the ice cream.

3. Transfer the churned ice cream to a lidded container, creating layers with additional Salara swirl if desired.

4. Freeze the ice cream for at least 3-4 hours or until it reaches the desired firmness.

MEASURES

1. **Volume Conversions:**
   o **1 cup = 240 milliliters**
   o **1 tablespoon = 15 milliliters**
   o **1 teaspoon = 5 milliliters**
   o **1 fluid ounce = 30 milliliters**
2. **Weight Conversions:**
   o **1 ounce = 28 grams**
   o **1 pound = 453 grams**
   o **1 kilogram = 2.2 pounds**
3. **Temperature Conversions:**
   o **Celsius to Fahrenheit: $F = (C \times 9/5) + 32$**
   o **Fahrenheit to Celsius: $C = (F - 32) \times 5/9$**
4. **Length Conversions:**
   o **1 inch = 2.54 centimeters**

- o 1 foot = 30.48 centimeters
- o 1 meter = 39.37 inches

5. **Common Ingredient Conversions:**

- o 1 stick of butter = 1/2 cup = 113 grams
- o 1 cup of flour = 120 grams
- o 1 cup of sugar = 200 grams

6. **Oven Temperature Conversions:**

- o **Gas Mark 1 = 275°F = 140°C**
- o **Gas Mark 2 = 300°F = 150°C**
- o **Gas Mark 4 = 350°F = 180°C**
- o **Gas Mark 6 = 400°F = 200°C**
- o **Gas Mark 8 = 450°F = 230°C.**

Made in the USA
Las Vegas, NV
26 November 2024

12682189R00075